Black Dimensions in Contemporary American Art

compiled and edited by

J. Edward Atkinson

A PLUME BOOK from
NEW AMERICAN LIBRARY
TIMES MIRROR
New York, Toronto and London

PLUME TRADEMARK REG. U.S. PAT. OFF. AND FOREIGN COUNTRIES
REGISTERED TRADEMARK—MARCA REGISTRADA
HECHO EN CLINTON, MASS., U.S.A.

Signet, Signet Classics, Signette, Mentor and Plume Books

are published *in the United States* by

The New American Library, Inc.,

1301 Avenue of the Americas, New York, New York 10019,

in Canada by The New American Library of Canada Limited,

295 King Street East, Toronto 2, Ontario,

in the United Kingdom by The New English Library Limited,

Barnard's Inn, Holborn, London, E.C. 1, England

First Printing, February, 1971

Printed in the United States of America

LIST OF ARTISTS AND PAINTINGS

PREFACE

Many of you reading this book for the first time will be seeking the answers to questions such as, "What is 'black art'?" and, "What is meant by the term a 'black aesthetic'?" If you expect to find in this visual survey a representative style that can be designated "black art," you will be disappointed. If you want to discern within these pages an aesthetic that is something other than the Europo-American one referred to in art texts and journals, again, you are searching in the wrong place.

This collection presents the forms and styles operative in the works of artists who have been assembled together, not because their creations are related by styles or form some kind of school, but because they happen to be Afro-American or artists of African descent. This is a visual survey. The point is worth repeating. The attempt is to give a general idea of the kinds of expressions that have emerged in contemporary black America. This book does not attempt to present one trend, one style or school: It is an arbitrary and fairly broad survey. In one sense this book is already obsolete because it is a survey.

Instead of trying to fit all of the art by those who happen to be black into one category or another, we need systematically to isolate those works that fall into one category from those that fit into another. In other words, we need to examine the kind of "trees" that are growing in the "forest" in order to assign proper names to all the various types represented and to determine whether there is an unclassified or new type present. The kind of voluminous approach that is being suggested has yet to be under-taken. Few nonblacks have either the historical vision or the intel-lectual appetite to deal seriously with the art of the American black in this way. Perhaps, and if for no other reason, it is because of the fantasy of an unrealized egalitarian ethic that haunts the Amer-ican imagination.

But when we ask, "What is the black aesthetic?" and, "What is black art?" we are talking about something other than what most art critics are prepared to deal with honestly at this point. The possibility of a black art/aesthetic is not a mainstream idea. It is not something nonblacks consider seriously. It is not something that is generally desired. It is a different and separate thing.

We are living, I believe, in a time when nonwhite people all over the globe are striving to develop and project an honest vision of their present collective conditions—spiritual, physical, and mental— and what they want their future to be. I see this as a transitional period in the development of an art and aesthetic for black people. It is a period when absolutes seem impossible. It is a period in which the art of black people is usually described as "protest," "propaganda," "sociological," "diverse," and "emotional" not- withstanding the fact that the same terms can be applied to Western art as well. All of these terms help to form the shield that hides the undercurrent of a different standard—a standard that is evolving among a large but scattered number of creators who may or may not be presented here.

These artists and thinkers are interested in the relationship be- tween aesthetics and ideology. Aesthetics and ideology seem to have converged at much the same time in the current works of many black artists. How do/should we account for this? It is be- cause a profound social consciousness has now been released in the black mind that different ideas about art and life are emerging. By briefly recalling some of the dynamics of the last twenty years, we can see that it is in the context of militant social developments in the United States and the world that we find the immediate sociopolitical roots of these surfacing ideas.

With the advent of the civil rights movement in the early fifties and the simultaneous drive for independence being made by Africans on the international stage, some black American artists began to focus (in their works as well as their thoughts and actions) on the position of black people internationally as well as domestically. The new confidence and pride that they expressed went much deeper and was more sustained than even that expressed by their predecessors—the Negro artists of the twenties and those of "The Harlem Renaissance." These younger artists had gotten even closer to their subjects and were on the move in step with the people as they marched through the streets of the fifties. This new-found social awareness led some artists to re-think the function of art in life. Some began to see art as functional in their lives and as a tool for physical and mental liberation. Others began seriously to explore the question of our relationship to Africa and the possibilities of residual African sensibilities. We must also recall that during this same period there was a great proliferation of historical, sociological, and cultural literature concerning the affairs of the black man and that bold new areas of political and social confrontations molded the realities of the sixties. Indeed, the new consciousness took a firm hold. Its artistic and social manifestations closed out the sixties and has opened the new decade with a heightened sense of political and social consciousness and commitment. If one doubts that a broad movement has evolved (one that is both aesthetic and ideological in nature) note how Larry Neal, a leading black poet-critic, recently announced the presence of a new art for his people:

> The Black Arts movement is rooted in a spiritual ethic. In saying that the function of art is to liberate Man, we propose a function for art . . . which is in keeping with our most ancient traditions and with our [contemporary] needs. Because at base, art is religious and ritualistic; and ritual moves to liberate Man and to connect him to the Greater Forces. Thus Man becomes stronger psychically, and is thus more able to create a world that is an extension of his spirituality—his positive humanity.
>
> The Black Arts movement preaches that liberation is inextricably bound up with politics and culture. The culture gives us a revolutionary moral vision and a system of values and a methodology around which to shape the political movement. When we say "culture," we do not merely mean artistic forms. We mean, instead, the values, the life styles, and the feelings of the people as expressed in everyday life. [1]

The need for new values and systems of thought is a foregone conclusion in the subbasement of America. Afro-American students, artists, writer-critics are excited about the possibilities of a systemized study of art and aesthetics from their own points of reference. They understand that it is in their own interest to lay the foundations for new and subjective impulses and interpretations of their art and life. They are focused upon and concerned

---

[1] Larry Neal, "Any Day Now: Black Art And Black Liberation," *Ebony* (August 1969), 54–55. Used by permission of the author.

with priorities of curricula, definitions, aesthetic theory, and revisionism. They see revisionism as part of the life blood of change as men have gone to the moon and 1984 is upon us! They are sending forth artist-liberators who are expounding the necessity to reduce the distance between art and life—artists and people, aesthetics and ideology—between themselves and their native vision.

—Edward S. Spriggs
Executive Director
The Studio Museum in Harlem

ACKNOWLEDGMENTS

We express sincere thanks for invaluable assistance in assembling and viewing the art in this collection to the family of the late James Porter and to Lucille Roberts, Washington, D.C., Margaret Burroughs, Chicago, Norah McNiven, Atlanta, and Beata Inaya and Dr. Leon Banks, Los Angeles.

Black Dimensions in Contemporary American Art was compiled and edited by J. Edward Atkinson, Senior Public Relations Supervisor, Carnation Company.

INTRODUCTION

During the years prior to 1960 few writers, critics, or students of art history bothered to consider the role of the black artist in American culture a subject worthy of scholarship. However, in 1936 Alain Locke's book *Negro Art: Past and Present* was published as a follow-up to his earlier book *The New Negro,* which had been published in 1925. Locke was looked upon as the spiritual father of the new invigorating movement later to be called "The Negro Renaissance." In both books his tone and spirit for the times mirrored his interest in a new appreciation for Africa and a return to what he referred to as the "ancestral arts." He strongly believed that knowledge of an African past would enhance the Afro-American's cultural literacy and awaken in him a sense of pride for his own cultural heritage.

Dr. Locke did not attempt to set forth in his new book *Negro Art: Past and Present* an ethos which enunciated the functional aesthetics of what he called Negro art. Instead, he was more interested in the general public being made aware of the role that the black artist had played in the making of American art. *Negro Art: Past and Present* was followed in 1940 by a book by the same author designed to show pictorially the black artist's perspective in world art. It is called *The Negro in Art* and describes black imagery, symbols, and content by artists of various ethnic origin.

The late James V. Herring, former chairman of the Department of Art, Howard University, also wrote enlightening articles attesting to the skills and craftsmanship of the black artist in the colonial period. But the most scholarly of such books on the subject of the black artist's contribution to American culture is *Modern Negro Art* written by James A. Porter in 1943. Porter was at that time a professor in the Department of Art at Howard University and is still regarded as the most authoritative spokesman on the subject of Afro-American art. Cedric Dover published *American Negro Art* in 1960 and made a contemporary evaluation of the black artist's work in the twentieth century.

The scholarly work of Alain Locke and James A. Porter was not continued until the year 1967 when black students began demanding changes in course curricula with specific reflections on the contributions of black Americans in the visual arts and in other areas of fine arts. It is against this background of interest and concern for the black man's cultural history in America that this summary of paintings is presented.

The intention of this publication is twofold. First, it attempts to show that a relevant number of black artists have always been conscious of their being apart from the mainstream of American art and have worked toward the creation of symbols that reflect the aesthetic needs of black Americans. This may be argued to be the closest manifestation toward the establishment of an ethos in black art. Secondly, it calls to our attention some of the problems generated by the attempts of contemporary philosophical thought to classify the art of black people in America without looking at the social, economic, and political conditions that have helped to make it a particular cultural entity to itself.

The verbal ethos which delineates black art from any other form of expression was established in the philosophy of Alain Locke. However, the black public, specifically an impatient young public, has turned to the artist and asked for signs and symbols in his work that reflect the specifics of Afro-American culture. A symbol is an accepted abbreviation of form which points beyond the ordinary perceptual world. With it, the viewer is made to understand an abstract form which is capable of transcending reality.

The artists whose works appear in this publication represent all sections of the United States. Their works show a variety of styles that are based in the various movements reflective of general trends in modern American art. These artists have a common history. Many of them have been exposed to the same life-styles and general cultural patterns, which cause the form and content of their work to be much the same. They have all been looked upon by sociologists as misfits in a technological society which emphasizes materialism instead of humanism. American artists have been traditionally viewed by a segment of the general public as visionary misfits endowed with magical intuition, capable of issuing forth talent at will. The black artist has not been exempted from this misconception.

It is still assumed by many people that the fine arts are forms which reflect man's leisure and consequently are synonymous with wealth. Since wealth in America is controlled by the white majority, one could readily assume that black artists do not participate in the creative process in the visual arts. But they do. The systematic denial of black artists' participation in the mainstream of American culture has been a deliberate act by art historians to affirm the black man's nonpresence or invisibility in American society. For this reason, one is often surprised to know that the history of the black man's participation in American culture as an artist goes back to colonial times.

The attitude concerning the black man as artist in American society is a sociological phenomenon based on the general desire to classify everything that involves human behavior. Since sociology is always mentioned in the context of the black man's survival as artist in the United States, one can narrowly escape the burden of a sociological perspective being imposed on the art of the American of African descent. Some observers believe that an artist's race or ethnic origin gives special meaning to the characteristics of his art. It is in this context that the recent use of the term "black art" is applicable to contemporary Afro-American art.

It is further necessary to mention sociology here in connection with art since in discussing the meaning of black art, the question of identity and aesthetics are often unknowingly combined. There is the sociological question, "What is it to be a black man in America?" and also the distinctly separate question, "What is it to be a black artist?". Making this distinction is a great help in understanding the meaning of the category "black art." It is likely within this context that the artist of the street, sometimes called "The black funky militant," feels that his art should be rightly termed "black art." His work, committed to propaganda and visual literacy, shows a literal interpretation of contemporary black life in America. This artist, unfortunately omitted from this publication, usually paints on walls, fences, and pavements. He does not feel the need for academic orientation and critical aesthetics that are bound within the western tradition of "good standards" in art. He is creating his "own thing" within the bounds of his own needs and is not asking for upper-societal judgments that are based in the aesthetics of western art. For this reason, we are unable to pass judgment on the value of his work as it is mentioned, this artist himself has exempted it from general aesthetics. He further argues that those artists and art historians who were trained prior to 1960 have a built-in aesthetic which creates a bias toward works that reflect a nonwestern tradition.

Perhaps this new form is being based in an ethos reflective of what is considered to be a societal need. Thus, the validity of the term "black art" as rightly argued by Jeff Donaldson, an articulate young spokesman for the black artists of the street, is not to be seen in the traditional concept of spiritual satisfaction through the experience of the symbol and what it means when viewed.

There exist perhaps two basic conflicting views concerning the creation of symbols and the purpose of art: one being that art's only commitment is to the form or symbol itself and that a work of art is an object to be perceived as a thing in itself, with little or no reference to other areas of experience. The other point of view being that art primarily is a means of expressing and communicating ideas and emotions.

Each of these perceptions has an inherent danger implied within it. The first perhaps promises to turn out cold and unfeeling art, completely divorced from any social reality even though symbols may be present. The second threatens to produce an art that must meet certain social needs. And, with the latter definition of art, people can too easily begin to dictate specific ideas and emotions that are to be expressed.

Both opinions have relevance to the black artist. It is clear that the artist must have a defined role as participant in his culture. In the African past, his art was in the service of the ruling family or was the basis for providing symbolic forms for ceremonial use.

But defining that role leads to definite difficulties. His role should not be so sterile as the first definition suggests, causing him to devote his entire life to the pursuit of an abstraction called "form," and completely divorcing himself from urgent social needs. But each artist must decide this for himself and plot his own role of involvement beyond form. Neither can one expect the Afro-American artist to become so involved in the social definition of being black in America that he allows his art to become a political tool. If a role for the artist is to be determined and if some effective guidelines are to be drawn up for art, then surely the only people qualified to do so are black artists. The two opposing views are implied in the question: How does one reconcile externally imposed artistic purposes with a complete internal freedom, when the social situation points up a definite need for some type of control?

Perhaps the best synthesis of the two opposing points of view must come from within each individual artist. Surely, no rigid external controls can be placed upon his creativity. He must be led by an intrinsic and internal force to create. But perhaps the difference in the art produced will come with a personal feeling of responsibility and commitment on the part of the artist as to his function and role within the society.

The black man's art in America, like his music, cannot be separated from his life. His art has evolved from his life-style and his will to survive. All that he perceives and makes with a medium will have his stamp on it. And for this reason, it may be argued that the art of the twentieth-century black artist is one which shows forms based on the expression of experiences that reflect a realistic portrayal of certain aspects of American life.

The dynamics of social protest and propaganda have played a vital role in twentieth-century Afro-American art. It is in this context that the black artist's work becomes a subcategory of American art taking into account like characteristics that reflect the state of being black in America in the twentieth century. If the experience of being black in America determines a black artistic style at all, it does not control the artistic expression in a restricted way. The variety of styles represented in this publication is a witness to this fact. An appreciation of the variety of styles found here is a prerequisite for examining the popular notion that the black experience in America by its very uniqueness produces a special art.

The diversity of styles presented in this publication does not dictate a homogeneous grouping; however, there is a unifying bond running through all of the works. The bond is formed by the emotional mood of many of the works presented as well as the common expression of experiences relating to the need to be expressive with a medium such as paint. A number of the artists represented are nationally known. Others less well known are seeing their work published for the first time. The styles represented range from the traditional portrait mastery of Aaron Douglas to the West African vignettes of John Biggers.

Since the black man in the United States is still in search of his identity as it relates to his cultural heritage, the absence of a distinct style of black art cannot be looked upon as a weakness of his culture. Instead one must realize that distinct symbolic forms are created out of societal needs that are acceptable for mass communication. In order to establish an acceptable style, forms must be created and used by the black community. This idea may account for the contention of some blacks that the only proper way to think about black art is to start from an altogether new base.

While the mainstream of contemporary American art has become progressively more concerned with form to the exclusion of objective content, art created by black Americans has tended to hold on to content as a vital part of its format. Content is a concept which is related to subject matter but different from it in that form in a work of art gives visual description to the object being depicted. Thus, content in the context of a black artist's work can be tied to a specific experience consistent with the uniqueness of being black in America. Since the artist's style determines and to a certain extent controls the form his art will take, style is an important factor in the art of the black American. It is surprising to some people to note the absence of the dynamic characteristics of

African art in the art of the black American. Yet, to force the iconography of African art on black artists would presuppose that their art is derived from art rather than from life itself. The black artist believes that the state of being black in America helps to create a unifying characteristic in his work that is based in the experiences of life instead of the systematic exploration of stylistic form.

The diversity of styles in this publication is unified by one factor, and it is this which further justifies bringing all of the works together in one book: all of the artists are black, living in America in the twentieth century, and feel the urge to be creative painters.

There is precedence for discussing contemporary black art in one of two ways: It can be looked upon as a separate form developed independently and distinctly apart from the larger context of twentieth-century American art or it can be looked upon as having derived its impetus directly from the study of American art. Neither of these points of view places contemporary art by black Americans in a proper perspective. It should not be denied that ethnic identification can play an important role in the making of artistic style. The Mexican muralists of this century have proven this point well. It is obvious that every aspect of an artist's background—his race, nationality, religion, family, and education— plays an important part in the formation of his art just as it helps in the shaping of his personality and expectations in life. What one is and what he has experienced in life will help to shape the form of his art as much as it will determine his life-style.

Twentieth-century American art has been characterized by a general move away from academic realism and social concern to abstract and nonobjective form. The same cannot be said of Afro-American art. While contemporary American art has become progressively more concerned with form to the exclusion of emotional or objective content, works created by black artists have generally emphasized content and are labeled by the critics as social realism. The emotional content of a painting results from the transformation of experiences into subject matter which becomes stable form. However, form can be created without emotional overtones being added. Such a tradition of painting devoid of content can be traced in this country. It is exemplified by the artist who paints in the tradition of the cubist and by the recent devotees of post-painterly abstractionism. This trend in America, art which comes from art rather than from life, can be seen in the works of some of the artists represented in this collection. The artists who follow this trend, however, are the exception rather than the rule in this regard.

The fact that most paintings by black artists do have emotional content is one aspect that forms an aesthetic bond linking them together. This shared characteristic helps unify the collection and shows that the significance of the black experience and all that it implies is the most likely explanation for the emotion which fills each canvas.

The whole argument of what black art is rests on the matter of the creation of black forms. Only those forms which by their very appearance are immediately identifiable as the products of the black artist clarify the symbolic meaning of black art. Hale Woodruff, respected black artist, historian, and critic, expressed the dilemma in this manner:

> If there is to be a Black Art, which is something made by a black artist, there must be certain outer manifestations so it can be identified as you can identify Oriental art or Pre-Columbian art or Eskimo art. I think the black artist is faced with the problem of almost working from scratch. If he doesn't resort to the traditional sources that are available, he has got to start from scratch. If he wants to produce a unique art form, he has got to ignore every other art form that has been used as a springboard. This is a tough job.[1]

There are qualities which define the American experience. Conflict and violence are notable among these. Naturally these qualities are reflective in the nation's art. The black experience is defined by these and by other special qualities unique to its suppression, struggle, passion, and soul force of revival and existence. These special qualities coupled with the artist's personal history and sensitivity to form are reflected in his paintings. There are works in this collection which illustrate this point. Lois Jones Pierre-Noël

---

[1]"The Black Artist in America: A Symposium," *Metropolitan Museum of Art Bulletin* (January 1969), 253–254.

has been profoundly influenced by the surrounding tempo and the mood of Haiti. The voodo motifs, bright colors, and lively spirit of her works are directly derived from an enchantment with that area. Other artists were deeply moved by a trip to Africa and have expressed an interest in the life and forms in African culture. John Biggers and Lucille Roberts are among these. Both artists have responded to the forms in African life which appealed to their stylistic interests. Lucille Roberts treats a traditional theme "Black Madonna" expressionistically, echoing a poetic rhythm of color and shapes that speak of the dynamics of semi-abstract form. There are times when an artist wishes to respond to what he calls "universal conditions" without localizing his art on the basis of his own race. In this case, style may be so personal as to discredit an ethnic label, but this does not destroy the relevant issues involved in the ultimate concern that the artist creates forms out of the depth of his personal experiences.

Charles White, one of the great voices among those black Americans who have for many years been the real interpreters of the Afro-American scene, in an interview appearing in the *Los Angeles Times,* said the following concerning his involvement with black imagery: ". . . I use Negro subject matter because Negroes are closest to me. But, I am trying to express a universal feeling through them, a meaning for all men . . . All my life, I have been painting a single painting. This does not mean that I am a man without anger . . . but what I pour into my work is a challenge of how beautiful life can be."[2]

Charles White's understanding of art goes beyond mere philosophy which takes into consideration man's benevolence or man's inhumanity to man. He is more concerned with the physical translation of form into spiritual matter which is meaningful to all who see it and to all who embrace the unity of life. Black life is closest to him, and he has responded warmly. It is in this sense that the artist's individuality comes forth when he shows his ability to create a physical embodiment of what is inside him.

[2]James A. Porter, "Charles White" (catalogue of the artist's works), The Art Gallery, Fisk University (1967), 9.

This writer does not contend that all black artists have embraced a common ethos which is reflective of a unified symbolic form. But it is safe to say that some have attempted it. There are those who feel that a black ethos in art is one which binds the spirit and dictates a common style which stifles individuality. Some artists feel that they are able to personalize their content beyond recognition and toward a visual iconography unrelated to ethnic or racial characteristics.

Recognition of the dilemma faced by the black artist in his attempt to define himself in American society helps us to understand the problem of isolating black art from general American art. Since he has been the victim of discrimination in all aspects of life, the black artist is forced to make a choice or strike a balance between two modes of expression: Is he to be first an artist and secondly a black American; or is he to be a black American responsive in his painting to the injustices, hypocrisies, and indignities suffered by the black man as a second-class citizen? Each artist responds to this dilemma in his own way depending on his own personal concerns and goals. The choice to be made is related to the artist's ability to personalize his own work. If he feels compelled to remove it from socially oriented issues, he is at liberty to do so. If he feels that he best represents himself through the portrayal of a sociopolitical literal orientation, then the propaganda of his work is his response as well as his motive expression.

This confrontation with artistic choice seems particularly important to black artists in the United States who are in the midst of a cultural revolution. In a trend following the general pattern of the Negro Renaissance, there is a great interest among the black population proclaiming black values in issues which tend to establish a social aesthetic that relies heavily on propaganda. There are those artists from the black community who have personalized their work so that one is not so much concerned about the color of the creative hand as he is about the symbol which provides inspiration for the observer.

Jacob Lawrence is probably the best known of all living black artists. Lawrence has searched for an African-based inspiration in his art, and his systematic use of what Professor Porter refers to as the "Negro theme" points to the fact that some artists are able to commit themselves to a personal graphic style which contains symbols distinctly racial in character and at the same time embrace the broad problems of humanity. For this reason, his work, though literally filled with black subjects, transcends the boundaries of time and place and puts black subjects in the category of universals.

Lawrence is more concerned with creating visual records which touch upon our ancestral interests. He is equally concerned with black history and the vital symbols that can be extracted from it. Many of his paintings contain some of the visual symbols associated with man's protest against the intolerable conditions that he faces from day to day, but they also reflect a segment of reality which ties our lives to history in a meaningful way. He distinguishes himself as an artist who is highly sensitive to the conditions of life that all mankind faces. He, like many other artists represented here, weathered the experience of growing up in a large city where social injustices were heaped upon him without any explanation as to why. These things contributed to his lifestyle, which became a determining factor in the life of a black man who wanted to become an artist. Consequently, here is a man whose tough times have contributed to his own salvation.

Professor Porter commented recently on the programatic stylism that social realism embodies when he talked about the possibility of the black artist returning to social realism as a means of translating those themes in his works that are necessarily black. It has been argued that Afro-American art, which has borne the label of social realism for a long period of time, has forced its own exclusion from shows which feature the most avant-garde methods in art. But all art that has been created by black artists has not fitted into the category of social realism. There are examples in this collection which present a concept of abstraction which is based in the contemporary feel for space and motion in a unique way. These works show the power of art in the universal sense.

There have been times when the black artist has been called upon to turn to Africa for those values which would stylistically cause his work to be set apart with a certain relevant meaning. After having been chosen the decided leader of the Negro Renaissance, Dr. Alain Locke wrote the following in an essay called *The African Legacy and the Negro Artist:*

> The constructive lessons of African Art are among the soundest and most needed of art today. They offset with equal force, the banalities of sterile imitative classicism and superficialities of literal realism. They emphasize intellectually significant form, abstract the balanced design, formal simplicity, the strained dignity and unsentimental emotional appeal. Moreover, Africa's art creed is beauty in use, vitally rooted in the crafts and uncontaminated with the blight of the machine. Surely the liberating example of such art will be as marked an influence in the contemporary work of Negro artists as it has been in that of the leading modernists: Picasso, Modigliani, Matisse, Epstein, Lipschitz, Brancusi, and others too numerous to mention. Indeed we may expect even more of an influence because of the deeper and closer appeal of African art to the artist who feels an historical and racial bond between himself and it. For him, it should not function as a novel pattern of eccentricity or an exotic idiom for clever yet imitative adaptation. It should act with all the force of a sound folk art, as a challenging lesson of independent originality or as clues to the re-expression of a half-submerged race soul. African art, therefore, presents to the Negro artist in the New World a challenge to recapture this heritage of creative originality, and to carry it to distinctive new achievement in a vital, new and racially expressive art.[3]

Those artists who have directed their work toward themes which echo an African heritage are responding to the sounds of cultural history. Others have chosen to concern themselves with the job of painting in abstract and expressionistic styles. Each artist has attempted to express in his own way a basic identity with the peculiar experiences of his life within the American complex. Many artists have argued in the tradition of Dr. Alain Locke that a real and vital racialism in art is a sign of objectivity and independence. Aaron Douglas found within the black experience a form of racial identity which communicates the historical meaning of Africa in the new world and strengthens its evolutionary consequences for world history. He was able to give stylistic meaning to forms in his work that were derivative of the African posture. His famous murals painted for the New York Public Library in Harlem

---

[3] Alain L. Locke, "The African Legacy and the Negro Artist" (exhibition of works of Negro artists), the Harmon Foundation, New York (1931), 11–12.

and for the Fisk University Library illustrate this point. It was through no stroke of luck that Douglas found himself involved in the execution of murals which tended to show the dignity of blackness as early as the 1920s. Instead, it was the genius of a bright young man who felt a close kinship to those neglected "primitive" forms which were still an obviously vital aspect of black life in America and particularly in the South. As a result of Douglas' keen sense of observation, a thorough knowledge of black history, and a steady hand of prophesy, a new way of seeing was opened up to black artists. The freshness of Douglas' approach to the question of a special black imagery substantiates the fact that an ethos is not a recent development.

The recent murals of the streets and the community wall projects show the desire by the black masses to have a special form in the visual arts peculiar to their own life-style. It can be rightly argued that music has fulfilled this vacuum in the Afro-American scene by synthesizing indigenous African folk elements with the sophisticated sounds of black life in America. But art is not a medium which survives the physical presence of body and soul. It is generally done with media that do not rely on one's physical body.

The art of black America has been a varied conglomeration of many interests, schools of thought, and modes of expression. However, the activism of the new generation of artists prophesies the beginning of a "grass roots" art which may be embedded in the soil of discontent with social injustice and deprivation, and it also speaks of an oncoming sign that black people in America no longer accept the idea that they must look to whites to be the interpreters of a culture in which they have only participated as observers.

Whereas it may rightly be argued that all black artists have not responded to a unifying symbol that sets their work apart from any other kind of art, it must be admitted that these artists have consistently been aware of the possible consequences of an aesthetic which would define their position of being black artists in a white racist society. Throughout the years, many well-known black artists have found it politically expedient to bind together to form organizations of unity to assure their own survival in the art world. As late as 1962 a group called Spiral, made up of black artists, functioned in New York City. Art critics and historians would argue that the ideal for art in America is "good art" just as there is the ideal for American citizenship to be comprehensive and bring into the fold all minority groups on the same respectful level of participation in society. But the general public must be made aware of the fact that the black artist has not thrust the burden of the new aesthetics upon himself. He was forced to take action on his own to see to it that the survival of his own art took place. Langston Hughes, poet laureate of black America, spoke succinctly to the point when he said in "Note on Commercial Theatre":

> . . . But someday somebody'll stand up and talk about me and write about me—Black and beautiful—and sing about me and put on plays about me! I reckon it'll be me myself yes, it'll be me.[4]

Many artists have begun to "sing" of themselves. Many others will come later. But their forms may be as varied in style and content as those we see represented here.

—**David C. Driskell**
Chairman, Art Department
Fisk University

[4] Langston Hughes, "Note on Commercial Theatre," in *Selected Poems of Langston Hughes,* 4th ed (New York: Alfred A. Knopf, 1968), 190.

Black Dimensions in Contemporary American Art

This volume affords an unprecedented national exposition for numerous black artists. It presents a unique opportunity for an infinite number of blacks and whites to develop a sensitivity to these painters—to view their vehicles of expression and to consider what they have to say.

We are deeply concerned that only a handful of black artists have exhibited in one-man shows at major museums across the country. We are equally dismayed by the fact that grade school through senior high level students in our inner cities invariably ask their teachers, after visiting these museums, "What about us, where are our artists?"

Thus, the collection presented here reflects a vast untapped wealth of talent—an exciting variety and quality of styles, a proud presentation of works by black artists from across the continent. The paintings are galvanized by feelings that mirror the diversity of the artists' individual fabrics, backgrounds, and techniques. Here is visual evidence that there are many black artists who rightfully deserve recognition from the art centers of America.

Black Dimensions in Contemporary American Art heralds the day when the genius of black art will find its way into the halls of uptown galleries.

—The Publishers

Benny Andrews

A native of Georgia, where he was born in 1930, Benny Andrews has studied at Fort Valley (Georgia) State College, the University of Chicago, and holds a B.F.A. from the Art Institute of Chicago. He has been shown in many group and one-man exhibitions, at the Forum Gallery, the New School for Social Research, the Paul Kessler Gallery (New York), the Detroit Institute of Art, the Philadelphia Academy of Art, the Brooklyn Museum, the New York World's Fair, the American Academy of Arts and Letters, the Art Students League (New York), the Minneapolis Institute of Art, Brooklyn College, the High Museum (Atlanta), the San Francisco Museum of Art, the Flint (Michigan) Institute of Art, the Museum of Modern Art (New York), and the Boston Museum of Fine Arts.

His work is represented in the collections of the Butler Institute of American Art (Youngstown, Ohio), the Museum of African Art (Washington, D.C.), the Slater Memorial Museum (Norwich, Connecticut), the La Jolla (California) Museum, and in the private collections of Joseph H. Hirshhorn and Raphael Soyer.

Benny Andrews was the recipient of a John Hay Whitney Fellowship and honorariums from Spelman College (Atlanta), Atlanta University, Bridgeport (Connecticut) University, and the Boston Museum of Fine Arts.

Andrews illustrated the book *I Am the Darker Brother* (1968) and has taught at California State College (Hayward), Queens College, and the New School for Social Research.

Benny Andrews, *Georgian Funeral,* 1965. Ink, 14 x 10 inches. Collection of Dr. and Mrs. Leon Banks, Los Angeles, California.

Calvin Bailey

Calvin Bailey is a West Coast artist who has had a long and varied career. Combining wit with perception, he has become one of America's leading caricaturists. His work has often been compared to that of Daumier in its social awareness. Using the quick-sketch technique, Bailey first gained recognition during the 1939–40 World's Fair in New York. He works primarily in black, sepia, and sanguine crayon, as well as in other media, and has drawn many of Hollywood's luminaries during the past thirty years.

Bailey has been a staff caricaturist for NBC-TV in Hollywood and has created and starred in his own San Francisco television show, the award-winning "Musical Sketch Book."

He has had frequent one-man shows, among them one at the League of Allied Arts, Los Angeles, California, and he is currently with the Burton Jay Art Center, Los Angeles.

His work is represented in many private collections.

Calvin Bailey, *The Old Man,* 1968. Oil, 48 x 17 inches.

Calvin Bailey, *Solo Session,* 1958. Oil, 24 x 30 inches.

John Biggers

John Biggers attended Hampton (Virginia) Institute and Pennsylvania State University, where he received the B.S., M.A., and D.Ed. degrees. He has been professor and head of the art department of Texas Southern University since 1949.

He was awarded a UNESCO Fellowship in 1957 to do an artist's study of life in West Africa. He received the Piper Professor Award (Distinguished Scholarship, State of Texas) 1964 and the Harbison Award for Distinguished Teaching, 1968.

He is a printmaker, painter, and sculptor with national recognition and has received a number of mural commissions. His works are to be found in museums and private collections throughout the country.

He is author of the book *Ananse: The Web of Life in Africa* (1962). Biggers was born in Gastonia, North Carolina, in 1924.

John Biggers, *Jubilee or Harvest Festival,* 1957. Casein and oil, $3\frac{1}{2}$ x 12 feet.

Arthur L. Britt, Sr.

Arthur Britt's work has been exhibited at the University of New Mexico, Lincoln University (Jefferson City, Missouri), Southern University (New Orleans), Stillman College (Tuscaloosa, Alabama), Indiana University, Atlanta University, and Louisiana State University. Mr. Britt has received awards from Atlanta University and West Virginia State College. His paintings are represented in the collections of Atlanta University, Lincoln University, Mississippi Valley State College, the University of New Mexico, and Stillman College.

He is currently chairman of the art department of Savannah State College.

Britt was born in 1934 in Cuthbert, Georgia. He has a B.S. from Alabama State College and an M.A. from the University of New Mexico. He writes of his work:

> I create in order that I might live.
> I live in order to create.
> My creations represent expression
> Of the Past, Present and Predicted Future
> Life of all mankind whether Black, White,
> Red or Yellow.

Arthur L. Britt, Sr., *Swamp Fire,* 1968. Oil, 24 x 30 inches.

Calvin Burnett

Calvin Burnett was born in Cambridge, Massachusetts, in 1921. He holds a B.F.A. from the Massachusetts School of Art, a B.S. in education from the Massachusetts College of Art, and an M.F.A. from Boston University. He has also studied at the Boston Museum and the Impressions Graphic Workshop (Boston). Burnett is currently a doctoral candidate at Boston University. He has taught and lectured throughout the United States and is a consultant to the Instrumentation Laboratory, Massachusetts Institute of Technology.

His work has been cited by Atlanta University, the Boston Printmakers, the Cambridge Art Association, the New England Print Competition, and Associated American Artists.

Burnett, who has also illustrated a number of books, has had his work exhibited at West Virginia State College, Lowell State College (Mass.), Children's Art Center (Boston), the Massachusetts Institute of Technology, the Brooklyn Museum, the National Academy of Design, the Library of Congress, Brandeis University (Waltham, Massachusetts), the Studio Museum in Harlem, and the Philadelphia Civic Center.

His work appears in the collections of the Boston Public Library, the Fogg Museum of Fine Arts (Cambridge, Massachusetts), Wellesley College, Howard University (Washington, D.C.), Atlanta University, and the Oakland Museum.

Calvin Burnett, *Insect,* 1963. Oil on canvas, 41 x 36 inches. Negro Collection, Atlanta University.

Margaret Taylor Goss Burroughs

Born in St. Rose, Louisiana, Margaret Burroughs came to Chicago at the age of five. She is a product of the Chicago public schools. She graduated from Chicago Teachers College and the Art Institute of Chicago and holds a master's degree in art education.

A teacher of art at DuSable High School in Chicago, Mrs. Burroughs has studied and painted in Mexico and at present is doing graduate work in art education at Columbia University. She is a founder of the South Side Community Art Center in Chicago and is the originator of Chicago's Lake Meadows Outdoor Art Fair, which she directs today.

She has won two national awards at the Annual Atlanta Exhibition of Negro Artists and has had articles published in the *Elementary English Journal* and the *Chicago Schools Journal*. Other published works include two juvenile books, *Jasper The Drummin' Boy* (1947) and *Did You Feed My Cow?* (1955).

Most recently Mrs. Burroughs served as art director and assistant in research for the Negro History Hall of Fame which was presented at the Chicago Coliseum by *The New Crusader* newspaper. Mrs. Burroughs is a founder and director of the Ebony Museum of Negro History and Art in Chicago.

Margaret Burroughs, *Blowing Bubbles,* 1968. Oil, 36 x 30 inches.

Arthur Carraway

Arthur Carraway studied at the Academy of Advertising Art and the California School of Fine Arts, both in San Francisco. His work has been exhibited at the San Francisco Art Association, the Los Angeles County Fair Graphic Art Annual, the Oakland Art Annual, the Flint (Michigan) Institute of Art, the San Francisco Museum of Art, the Black Arts Festival (Walnut Creek, California), and the University of the Pacific (Stockton, California). He has received awards from the Los Angeles County Fair, the Oakland Art Annual, and the San Francisco Art Commission Annual Art Festival.

Carraway has been published in *Black Artists on Art* (1969), edited by Dr. Samella S. Lewis and Ruth Waddy, and in the magazine *Black Dialogue*.

Arthur Carraway, *Fetish Form Series #IV,* 1969. Oil on canvas, 20 x 36 inches.

Bernie Casey

The son of a mine laborer, Bernie Casey was born in Wyco, West Virginia, in 1939.

He received his B.F.A. and M.F.A. from Bowling Green State University (Bowling Green, Ohio), where he was All-American halfback. In 1961 Casey was the first draft choice for the San Francisco Forty-Niners, a team for which he starred during his six seasons in the National Football League. In 1967 he was traded to the Los Angeles Rams. After he retired from professional football in 1968, Casey began to pursue two careers, one in painting and one in films. He has had considerable success in both and has published a book of poetry as well. A multitalented artist, Casey has his work much sought after by collectors and is considered highly by critics here and abroad.

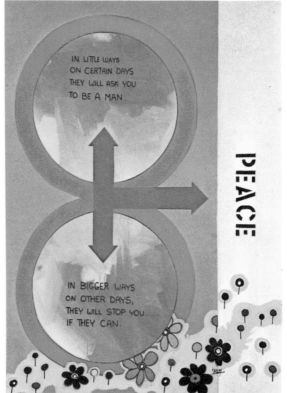

Bernie Casey, *In Little Ways,* 1969. Acrylic on canvas, 30 x 40 inches.

Bernie Casey, *You Can Win the Game If It's Your Turn,* 1967. Oil, 48 x 36 inches. Collection of Mr. & Mrs. Jules Glazer, Beverly Hills, California.

Dan Concholar

Dan Concholar is presently drawing and painting teacher at the Watts Towers Art Center. He studied at Phoenix College and Pasadena City College. Concholar has had his work exhibited in the Arizona State Fair (first prize, graphics, 1959; first prize, painting, 1969), the Phoenix Art Museum, the Udinotti Gallery (Scottsdale, Arizona), and the Brockman Gallery (Los Angeles). He was born in San Antonio, Texas, in 1939.

Dan Concholar, *Fact of Man,* 1965. Oil on canvas, 36 x 40 inches.

Dan Concholar, *Series of Africa #2,* 1969. Acrylic, 30 x 36 inches. Collection of Naomi Caryl Hirshhorn.

Mary Reed Daniel

A native of East St. Louis, Illinois, Mary Daniel has had her work exhibited in the Midwest since 1960, winning awards and honorable mentions at various art fairs.

Mrs. Daniel has experimented in various mediums but is particularly noted for her watercolors and pen-and-ink drawings.

Among the exhibitions where she has been represented have been those at Lincoln University (Jefferson City, Missouri), Atlanta University, the South Side Community Art Center and McCormick Place (Chicago), and the University of Wisconsin. Rockford (Illinois) College, the African Art Museum (Chicago), and the Illinois Bell Telephone Company have purchased her paintings for their permanent collections. Mrs. Daniel's work has also found its way into private collections in the United States, Canada, and Europe.

Mary Reed Daniel, *A Friend*, 1969. Acrylic, 11 x 15 inches.

Alonzo Joseph Davis, Jr.

Alonzo Davis has been consultant to the High School Art Work-shop, Black Students Union, and the Art Mobile (Los Angeles City School District). He is the owner and art director of the Brockman Gallery, which promotes and features minority artists, and is consultant to Gallery Negra. His work has appeared in the Brockman Gallery, Dialogue Through Art Exhibitions, Occidental College, and Gallery Negra (Los Angeles), and the Laguna Beach (California) Art Association.

He was born in Tuskegee, Alabama, in 1942, studied at Los Angeles City College, and received a B.A. in art from Pepperdine College, Los Angeles. He has done postgraduate work in art and education at the University of Southern California, the University of California at Los Angeles, and the Otis Art Institute of Los Angeles County.

Alonzo J. Davis, Jr., *Black Modern Dance,* 1969. Print, 36 x 36 inches. Reprinted courtesy of the Brockman Gallery, Los Angeles, California.

Alonzo J. Davis, Jr., *Heart Dance,* 1969. Print, 36 x 36 inches. Reprinted courtesy of the Brockman Gallery, Los Angeles, California.

Juette Johnson Day

Born and educated in Richmond, Virginia, Juette Day received her B.S. degree from Virginia Union University in Richmond. She has studied since at Columbia University and at Ohio State University, from which she received her M.A. in fine arts.

Mrs. Day has taught art for twenty years in the Washington Public Schools and at District of Columbia Teachers College.

In 1947 she won the Delver Woman's Club Award for first prize in its art show.

In a show of the work of Washington art teachers her paintings received a special commendation.

A one-woman show of her thesis paintings was held at Ohio State University in 1954. Another one-woman show was held in 1967 at the Potter's House Gallery, Washington, D.C., the paintings for which were selected and approved by the National Council of the Arts. A third show was held at the Richmond Public Library in 1967.

Two of her paintings travel currently with the College Arts Society, a project begun under the auspices of the art department of Howard University, Washington, D.C.

Juette Day, *Cathedral*, 1968. Oil, 28 x 36 inches.

Juette Day, *Plight*, 1969. Oil, 50 x 62 inches.

Aaron Douglas

Retired chairman of the art department at Fisk University in Nashville, Tennessee, Aaron Douglas is a native of Kansas. He was awarded fellowships from the Rosenwald Fund and the Barnes Foundation and a scholarship in the Winold Reiss School of Art (New York). Douglas also studied at L'Académie Scandinave in Paris under Frieze and Despiau. He received his bachelor of fine arts degree in 1922 from the University of Nebraska.

His murals appear in the Harlem Branch of the New York Public Library, Fisk University, and Bennett College, Greensboro, North Carolina. Douglas' book illustrations include those in *God's Trombones* by James Weldon Johnson and *Black Magic* by Paul Morand. He has had exhibitions at the Caz-Delbo Galleries (New York), the Brooklyn Museum, the Finlay Galleries, the University of Nebraska, and in numerous other museums and galleries throughout the United States.

Aaron Douglas, *Portrait of Dr. Mary McCleod Bethune,* 1969. Oil, 4 x 5 feet. Reprinted courtesy of Minneapolis Public Schools.

David C. Driskell

David Driskell was born in 1931 in Eatonton, Georgia. He holds a B.A. in fine arts from Howard University and an M.F.A. from the Catholic University (both in Washington, D.C.). He has studied at the Skowhegan School of Painting and Sculpture (Maine) and at the Rijksbureau voor Kunsthistorisches Documentatie (The Hague, Holland).

Among his fellowships are a Danforth Foundation Special Study Grant (1961–2), a Rockefeller Foundation Grant (1964), a Museum Donor Award from the American Federation of Arts (1962), a Harmon Foundation Special Award (1964), and an Honorable Mention in Graphic Art from the Corcoran Gallery (1965).

Driskell's work has been exhibited at the Corcoran Art Gallery, the Howard University Gallery of Art (Washington, D.C.), the Lincoln University Gallery (Jefferson City, Missouri), the National Museum, the Smithsonian Institute, the Rhodes National Gallery (Salisbury, Rhodesia), the King George VI Gallery (Port Elizabeth, South Africa), the Oakland Art Museum, and the White House.

Driskell is represented in *Who's Who in American Art* (1962), Cedric Dover's *American Negro Art* (1960), Frederick Wight's *American Negro Art* (1966), and *Prints by American Negroes* (1967).

His works are in the collections of the Skowhegan School, Howard University Gallery of Art, the Corcoran Art Gallery, the Danforth Foundation, the Smithsonian Institution, the United States Embassy in Copenhagen, and in many private collections.

Driskell is currently professor and chairman of the Department of Art, Fisk University, Nashville, Tennessee.

David C. Driskell, *Reflection & Dream*, 1968. Gouache, 18½ x 26 inches. On loan from the artist.

Eugenia V. Dunn

In 1959 Eugenia Dunn retired from teaching to begin a career as a professional artist. She had been a professor of biology at Spelman College (Atlanta), assistant professor and chairman of Science and Mathematics Department, Bethune-Cookman College (Daytona Beach, Florida), and assistant dean of women, Spelman College, until 1959.

Her work has been included in the exhibitions of Atlanta University, Spelman College, public schools in Tuskegee, Alabama, the Kentucky State Fair, Howard University (Washington, D.C.), the Cronow Gallery (Louisville), the Cultural Exchange Exhibition (Houston), Morgan State College (Baltimore), the Housewives League (Louisville), and the American Professional Artists League's Annual National Art Week program.

Miss Dunn was born in Henderson, Kentucky. She graduated from Louisville Municipal College of the University of Louisville with a B.S. in biology with honors and from Atlanta University with an M.S. in biology. Miss Dunn has done postgraduate work in science education at the University of Michigan.

She is represented in Cedric Dover's *American Negro Art* (1960) and the National Conference of Artists' *Print Portfolio of Negro Art* (1963).

Eugenia V. Dunn, *Gosman's Dock*, 1968. Oil, 36 x 30 inches.

Marion Epting

After serving in the United States Navy, Marion Epting entered Otis Art Institute of Los Angeles County and was graduated with a master of fine arts degree in May, 1969. He is also a graduate of Los Angeles City College.

His work is in the permanent collections at Otis Art Institute, University of California, Los Angeles, San Jose State College, Denison University (Granville, Ohio), and the Seattle Art Museum, and in the private collections of Bernie Casey, Dorothy Chandler, Claude Booker, Ruth Stoehr, and James Bates.

Epting has been the recipient of many awards, among them the First San Diego National Invitational Print Exhibition, Potsdam Prints (Potsdam, New York), Northwest Printmakers (Seattle), Del Mar (California) Invitational, and Portland (Oregon) Art Museum.

The artist was born in Forrest, Mississippi, in 1940.

Marion Epting, *Klunk Boom,* 1969. Color etching, 39 x 26 inches. Collection of Mrs. Beata Inaya, Los Angeles. Reprinted courtesy of the Mafundi Institute, Watts, California.

Marion Epting, *Hiku,* 1969. Color etching, 18 x 18 inches. Collection of the Honorable Alan Sieroty, Beverly Hills, California.

Russell Gordon

Russell Gordon is a native of Philadelphia and holds a B.F.A. (1962) from the Tyler School of Fine Arts, Philadelphia, an M.S. and an M.F.A. (1966, 1967) from the University of Wisconsin. He is currently associated with the University of California, Berkeley.

His work has appeared in a number of shows, among them the Northwest Printmakers International (Seattle), the Pennsylvania Academy of Fine Arts (Philadelphia), the Philadelphia Print Club, the Society of American Graphic Artists (New York), the United States "Art in the Embassies" program, the University of Minnesota, and DePauw University (Greencastle, Indiana).

The artist is represented in the collections of the Philadelphia Museum of Art, the Carnegie Corporation of New York, Duke University (Durham, North Carolina), the New Jersey State Museum (Trenton), the Friends Neighborhood Guild of Philadelphia, and the Philadelphia Board of Public Education.

Russell Gordon, *Kaleido-scopic Series #2,* 1968. Acrylic, 48 x 84 inches. On loan from the artist.

Russell Gordon, *Kaleidoscopic Series #1,* 1968. Acrylic, 60 x 84 inches.

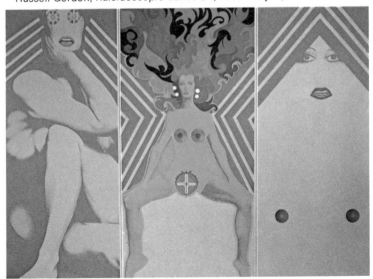

David Hammons

David Hammons was born in 1943, in Springfield, Illinois. He studied at Los Angeles City College, Los Angeles Trade Technical College, Chouinard Art Institute (Los Angeles), and Otis Art Institute of Los Angeles County. His work has been exhibited in the Inglewood (California) Library, the Laguna Beach (California) Art Association, and by the National Council of Jewish Women. Hammons has published in *Wilson Library Bulletin* and has lectured at California State College (Dominguez Hills).

David Hammons, *Back to Black*, 1969. Monoprint, 34 x 42 inches.

David Hammons, *Flag Day*, 1968. Monoprint, 32 x 42 inches. Collection of the Honorable Alan Sievoty, Beverley Hills, California.

Phillip J. Hampton

Works by Phillip Hampton have been exhibited at such galleries as the William Rockhill Nelson Gallery, the Mid-American Gallery (Kansas City, Missouri), the Dulin Gallery (Knoxville, Tennessee), the Savannah Art Association. He has had one-man shows at Lincoln University (Jefferson City, Missouri), Savannah State College, and Florida A&M University (Tallahassee). His work has appeared nationally and regionally and has won best-in-the-show, first, and several purchase prizes. More than 100 of his paintings and murals are in several colleges, public schools, businesses, and private collections.

Hampton is listed in *Who's Who in American Art, The Register of United States Living Artists,* and *American Negro Art* by Cedric Dover. He holds membership in several national, international, and local organizations. Hampton was selected by the student chapter of Savannah State College of the National Association as Outstanding Teacher of the Year in 1965. He has been awarded plaques and certificates by local and national organizations for his contributions to art and the promotion of art.

Hampton was born in Kansas City, Missouri, in 1922. He attended Citrus Junior College (Glendora, California), Kansas State College, Drake University (Des Moines, Iowa), Kansas City University, and the Kansas City Art Institute, where he received his B.F.A. and M.F.A. degrees in 1951 and 1952. He is presently associate professor of art at Southern Illinois University.

Phillip J. Hampton, *A Weekend Song,* 1968. Oil, 42 x 42 inches. Collection of Colonel L. J. Mantoux (USAF Ret.), Savannah, Georgia.

Marvin Harden

Marvin Harden's paintings can be found in the collections of the Museum of Modern Art, Metromedia, the Westside Jewish Community Center (Los Angeles), the San Diego Jewish Community Center, and in many private collections.

Harden was born in Austin, Texas, and holds a B.A. in fine arts and an M.A. in creative painting from U.C.L.A.

He has had exhibitions at the Philadelphia Civic Center Museum, the Los Angeles County Museum, the La Jolla Museum, Occidental College (Los Angeles), Los Angeles City College, the Sixteenth All-City Art Festival, Los Angeles, the San Francisco Museum of Art, and the New York World's Fair American Express Pavilion. His work has been represented in the Minneapolis Institute of Arts and the University of California at Los Angeles touring exhibitions.

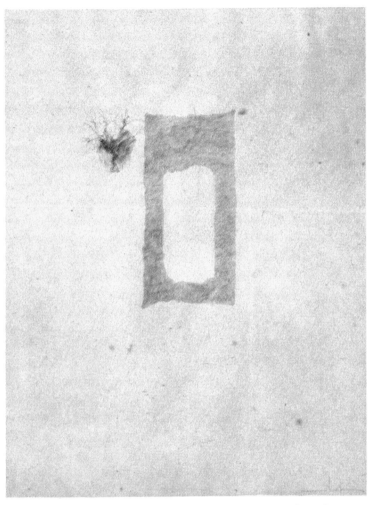

Marvin Harden, *Perfectly Logical & Inevitable,* 1967. Pencil, 21¼ x 17¾ inches. Collection of Dr. and Mrs. Leon O. Banks, Los Angeles, California.

Wilbur Haynie

Wilbur Haynie was born in 1929 in Camden, Arkansas. He received an M.F.A. from the Otis Art Institute of Los Angeles County. He has also studied at the Dallas County Museum of Fine Arts, the School of Allied Arts (Glendale, California), and Wiley College (Marshall, Texas).

He has received awards from the Newport Beach (California) Annual Exhibit, the All-City Art Festival (Los Angeles), the Southern California Exhibit, and the Watts Festival (Los Angeles).

Haynie's work has been exhibited at the Los Angeles Art Association, the Los Angeles County Fair, the California State Fair, the Houston Museum of Fine Art, the San Diego Museum of Art, the Long Beach Museum of Art, the Los Angeles County Museum, the University of California Art Galleries (Los Angeles), and the Watts Festival.

His work is represented in the collections of the Fine Art Patrons of Newport Harbor (California), the Otis Art Institute, the Pasadena Art Museum, and in numerous private collections.

Wilbur Haynie, *Untitled,* 1963. Oil, 36 x 48 inches. Collection of the Pasadena Art Museum, Pasadena, California.

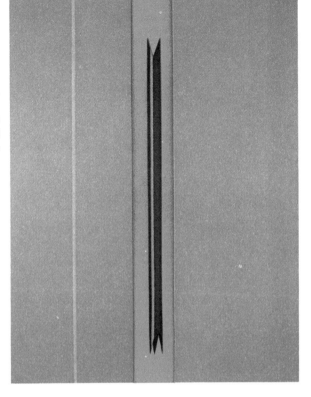

Wilbur Haynie, *Untitled,* 1968. Oil, 60 x 72 inches. Collection of Mrs. Beata Inaya, Los Angeles, California.

Richard Hunt

Richard Hunt's work has been exhibited in one-man shows at the Alan Gallery (New York), the B. C. Holland Gallery (Chicago), and the University of Tulsa. He has also been shown at the Museum of Modern Art, the International Exhibition of Painting and Sculpture at Carnegie Institute of Technology (Pittsburgh), the Whitney Museum of American Art, the Solomon R. Guggenheim Museum, the Seattle World's Fair, the Art Institute of Chicago, and the Felix Landau Gallery (Los Angeles). His paintings are in the permanent collections of many art museums in the United States and Europe.

Hunt was born in Chicago in 1935. He received a B.A.E. from the Art Institute of Chicago. His awards include the James Nelson Raymond Foreign Traveling Fellowship, a Guggenheim Fellowship, and a Tamarind Fellowship.

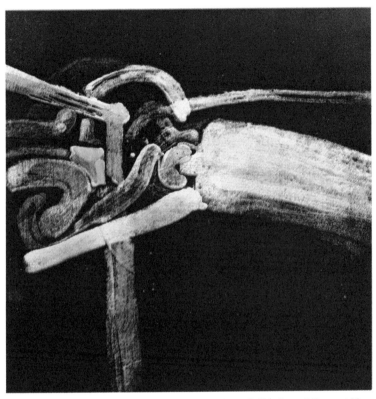

Richard Hunt, *Untitled,* 1965. Oil, 15 x 15 inches. Collection of Dr. and Mrs. Leon O. Banks, Los Angeles, California.

Barbara J. Jones

Born in Chicago in 1938, Barbara J. Jones holds a B.A. degree from Howard University (Washington, D.C.) and a B.F.A. from the Art Institute of Chicago. Miss Jones is currently studying at the Institute of Design, Illinois Institute of Technology (Chicago).

Her awards include the Chicago Art Society Scholarship and First Prize Print Award in *Black Expressions* (1969).

She has had one-woman shows at the 353 East Gallery, the Lakeside Gallery, the Hyde Park Savings and Loan, and the Afam Gallery (all Chicago). Her work has also appeared in group shows and exhibitions at the University of Notre Dame (South Bend, Indiana), the Chicago Public Library, and the Old Town Art Fair, the Afro Arts Theatre, the African Lion, the Southside Community Art Center, and the Allan Frumkin Gallery (all Chicago).

Barbara J. Jones, *Your Brother's Keeper,* 1968. Silk screen print, 24 x 24 inches.

Lois Mailou Jones (Mrs. V. Pierre-Noël)

Lois Mailou Jones (Mrs. Veroniaud Pierre-Noël) became in 1941 the first black artist to receive the Robert Woods Bliss Landscape Prize for Oil Painting at the Corcoran Gallery of Art. Her fifteen other awards include the Diplôme and Decoration de l'Ordre National from the Government of Haiti (1934), the Societé des Artistes Français (1966), the Franz Bader Award for Oil Painting, Washington Society of Artists (1962), and the John Hope Award, Atlanta University (1949).

She was born in Boston and is a graduate of the Boston Museum of Fine Arts. She holds a B.A. from Howard University (Washington, D.C.) and has studied at the Académie Julien in Paris. Miss Jones is currently professor of design and watercolor painting in the College of Fine Arts at Howard University.

Her one-woman shows include exhibitions at the Pan American Union (Washington, D.C.), the Salon des Artistes Français (Paris), the Rhodes National Gallery (Salisbury, Rhodesia), the King George VI Art Gallery (Port Elizabeth, South Africa), the National Academy of Design (New York), and the National Museum of Art (Washington, D.C.).

Miss Jones' work appears in the permanent collections of the Corcoran Art Gallery, the Howard University Gallery of Art, the Schomburg Collection in Harlem, the Walker Art Museum of Bowdoin College (Brunswick, Maine), Atlanta University, and the University of Punjab, Pakistan.

References to her work are included in *The Negro in Art* by Alain Locke, *Modern Negro Art* by James Porter, *The Negro in American Culture* by Margaret Butcher, *American Negro Art* by Cedric Dover, *Who's Who in American Women,* as well as in many other American and foreign publications.

Lois Mailou Jones (Mrs. V. Pierre-Noël), *Challenge*, 1969. Collage, 30 x 39 inches.

Lois Mailou Jones, *Vèvè Vodou III*, 1968. Oil-collage, 30 x 38½ inches.

Jack Jordan

Jack Jordan's creations have been exhibited in twenty-two states: eighteen one-man exhibitions, numerous cash commissions, fourteen invitational exhibitions, and fourteen art museums. He has received over thirty art awards in local, regional, national, and integrated competitions. Along with other leading American artists, Jordan exhibited in the New York City Architectural League, the National Sculpture Society, The Internationale Buchkunst Austellung (Leipzig, Germany), the Providence (Rhode Island) Gallery, the Philadelphia Commerical Art Museum, the State University of Iowa Art Gallery, the Atlanta University Art Gallery, the Louisiana State University Invitational Art Exhibition, the Oklahoma Art Center, the Information and Education Center (Ft. Campbell, Kentucky), the Walker Art Center (Minneapolis), Texas Southern University Art Gallery, New Vistas of American Art at Howard University (Washington, D.C.), Emancipation Centennial National Art Exhibition (Chicago), the Beaux Arts Guild (Tuskegee, Alabama), Lincoln University Art Gallery (Jefferson City, Missouri), and the El Mira Art Gallery (Pismo Beach, California). Abroad, three of his prints traveled with exhibits in Leningrad, Baku, Alma-Ata, Prague, and Moscow.

Jack Jordan is included in *Who's Who in American Education,* a print portfolio by Negro artists, National Conference of Artists, *Great Negroes Past and Present, Prints by American Negro Artists,* and Delta Phi Delta National Honorary Art Fraternity.

Jordan was born in Wichita Falls, Texas, and has an A.B. in art from Langston University (Langston, Oklahoma), an M.A. in art education from Iowa University, and an M.F.A. in sculpture from the State University of Iowa. He has studied sculpture and graphics at Oklahoma University.

Jack Jordan, *Soul Family,* 1969. Oil, 12 x 30 inches.

Jack Jordan, *Negro, Banjo, and Soul,* 1968. Oil, 24 x 30 inches.

Lemuel M. Joyner

A native of Nashville, Tennessee, Lemuel Joyner was born in 1928, and received both his B.F.A. and M.F.A. from the University of Notre Dame in Indiana. He has worked as an artist-designer for St. Christopher's workshop in Bremen, Indiana, which designs and manufactures church furnishings, and for the past four years, he has been a member of the faculty at Saint Mary's College, Notre Dame, Indiana. He is currently an associate professor of art and a special assistant to the president of the college in the area of Inter-Cultural Development, with special responsibility for academic and social programs for black students and other ethnic minorities. Joyner has this to say of his work:

> The title of the painting is a summation of personal values and vision, not only as they necessarily pertain to myself but as they impinge upon the society in which I live.
>
> The judgment relates to my past insofar as, out of its chaotic indefiniteness, I had finally achieved a kind of definition; having had an education, I assumed that hard work backed by determined purpose would inevitably bring the rewards my career had to offer. The future, however, indicated a judgment harsher than the naïvité of the past: although I was ready for society, it became quite clear that society had not prepared itself to take me into its account.

Lemuel M. Joyner, *Judgment,* 1960. Oil, 19 x 32 inches.

Henri Linton

Henri Linton is a native of Alabama, born in 1944. He has studied at the Columbus College of Art and Design (Columbus, Georgia), the University of Alabama, and the Boston University School of Fine and Applied Arts. He has received awards and scholarships from Boston University, Atlanta University, and the Columbus Art League. His work has been exhibited at Stillman College (Tuscaloosa, Alabama), Atlanta University, Ohio State University, and the Columbus (Ohio) Gallery of Fine Arts. Henri Linton is currently teaching at Arkansas A.M.&N. College in Pine Bluff, Arkansas.

Henri Linton, *Alone,* 1968. Oil on canvas, 47 x 58 inches. Reprinted courtesy of Negro Collection, Atlanta University.

Jimmie Mosely

After spending two years in the U.S. Navy, Jimmie Mosely entered Florida A.&M. College in 1947, then transferred to Texas Southern University where he was the first student to graduate with a bachelor of fine arts degree (1952).

Mosely has taught at Lincoln University (Jefferson City, Missouri), Texas Southern University, and the University of Maryland. He has done advanced degree work at Pennsylvania State and Rutgers Universities.

His awards include a third prize in paints, Atlanta University National Art Show in 1954 for his painting, "Korean Prisoners"; first prize in water color painting, Atlanta University National Art Show in 1963 for "Johannesburg"; first prize in water color painting in Atlanta University National Art Show in 1965 for "Protest." Mosely was a member of the Committee to Improve Art in Negro Colleges at the Department of Fine Arts Indiana University (Indianapolis). He has been president of the National Conference of Artists. He is now director of art education at Maryland State College.

Mosely was born in 1927 in Lakeland, Florida.

Jimmie Mosley, *Waiting to Vote,* 1968. Watercolor, 24 x 30 inches.

Ademola Olugebefola

Born in St. Thomas, Virgin Islands, in 1941, Ademola Olugebefola graduated from the Fashion Institute of Technology (New York) with advanced training in fashion design. He has studied advertising and commercial art with The House of Umoja Cultural Exchange Program in New York, and is presently its executive director.

Olugebefola is mainly self-taught in the fine arts. His works are in oil, acrylic, watercolors, collage, woodcutting, lithography, drawing, and sculpture.

Olugebefola's work is presently in the permanent collections of Nyumba Ya Sanaa, Pamoja Galleries, Gary Arts Ltd., the Key, Malikah Galleries, DWS Contemporary Furniture Inc., Pyramid Gallery, and Bestu Contemporary Unlimited, as well as in numerous private collections throughout the United States.

His one-man and group shows have been many. They include those at the New York Bank For Savings, the Bowery Savings Bank, the Afro-Arts Cultural Center, the Countee Cullen Library, the Kenwood Reters Furniture Galleries, the Truth, Woodstock and Statler Hilton Hotels (all in New York City), the State University of New York at Stony Brook, Brooklyn Community College, and the Bronx Council of the Arts.

Deeply concerned with the issues and developments that affect humanity, Olugebefola is currently working on a series of paintings, sculpture, and woodcuts which he calls "Mask of the Sacred Poro Society" and "Burden of Injustice" in limited editions.

In recent shows, he has exhibited at the Corcoran Gallery, the Brooklyn Museum, Bronx Community College, Lincoln University (Pennsylvania), and the African American Art Festival in Delaware.

Olugebefola is one of the pioneers of the contemporary black art movement. His lectures on traditional African art forms and their contemporary manifestation have won wide acclaim. His art form is considered as an important influence and catalyst in the black art world.

Ademola Olugebefola, *Olori My Son,* 1969. Acrylic on posterboard, 22 x 28 inches. Reprinted courtesy of the Weusi Nyumba Ya Sanaa Gallery, New York.

John Outterbridge

John Outterbridge was educated at North Carolina A.&T. University, the American Art Academy (Chicago), the Chicago Academy of Art, and the Art Center School of Design (Los Angeles). He has had many group exhibitions, among them at the Watts Summer Festival of Art, the Brockman Gallery (Los Angeles), the Oakland Museum, the Long Beach Museum, and the Pasadena Artists Association.

Mr. Outterbridge is currently lecturing on Afro-American History at California State College (Dominguez Hills).

John Outterbridge, *Mood Ghetto,* 1967. Oil, 12 x 18 inches. Collection of Mrs. Sylvia Miller, Los Angeles.

John Outterbridge, *The Old Folks,* 1968. Oil, 24 x 21 inches. Collection of Mrs. Sylvia Miller, Los Angeles.

William Pajaud

William Pajaud was born in New Orleans, Louisiana, in 1925. He has a B.A. from Xavier University (New Orleans) and has studied further at the Chouinard Art Institute (Los Angeles).

His work has been exhibited at the Los Angeles County Art Institute, the Los Angeles County Museum, Atlanta University, the Pasadena Art Museum, the De Young Museum (San Francisco), Wisconsin University, Los Angeles City College, and the Palm Springs Museum. He has been the recipient of the Atlanta University Annual Award and the Los Angeles Westside Jewish Community Center Annual Award. His one-man shows have appeared at the Esther Robles Gallery (Los Angeles), the Heritage Gallery (Los Angeles), the Esquire Theatre (Pasadena), and the Emerson Gallery (Encino).

Pajaud's work is represented in the collections of Sammy Cahn, Harry Karl, Charles T. Coiner, Norton Simon, the American Artists Group, and Atlanta University.

William Pajaud, *Family Circle,* 1969. Oil, 24 x 30 inches. Reprinted courtesy of the Heritage Gallery.

James D. Parks

A painter and art historian, James D. Parks was born in St. Louis. He holds a B.S. in art from Bradley University (Peoria, Illinois) and an M.A. from the State University of Iowa. He has studied at the Chicago Art Institute and traveled and painted in Mexico and Europe.

Parks' work is represented in the permanent collections of Howard University (Washington, D.C.), Atlanta University, Lincoln University (Jefferson City, Missouri), Texas Southern University, and the Springfield (Missouri) City Art Museum. He is a cofounder of the National Conference of Artists. At present he is chairman of the art department, Lincoln University.

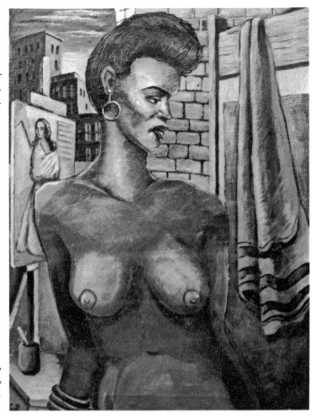

James D. Parks, *Artist Model,* 1960. Oil, 20 x 26 inches.

James D. Parks, *Missouri Village,* 1965. Watercolor, 20 x 15 inches.

Delilah W. Pierce

Delilah Pierce was born in Washington, D.C. and holds a B.S. from Howard University (Washington, D.C.) and an M.A. from Teachers College, Columbia University. She has done postgraduate work at the University of Pennsylvania, New York University, the University of Chicago, and the Museum of Modern Art. Her work has been exhibited at the Lois Jones Studio and the Margaret Dickey Gallery (Washington, D.C.); Atlanta University; the Corcoran Gallery of Art Area and Traveling Exhibits; the Baltimore Museum; Howard University, Catholic University, and the Artists Mart (all in Washington, D.C.).

Mrs. Pierce has been the recipient of the Agnes Meyer Summer Traveling Fellowship (1962) and awards from the American Federation of Art Museums, the Corcoran Gallery, and the National Sorority of Phi Delta Kappa.

She is listed in Cedric Dover's *American Negro Art, Washington Artists Today,* and *Who's Who in American Education.*

Her work is in the collection of the Howard University Gallery of Art and in many private collections.

Mrs. Pierce is currently an assistant professor in the art department of District of Columbia Teachers College.

Delilah W. Pierce, *Tradermen—Khartoum, Sudan,* 1952. Oil, 24 x 42 inches.

Delilah W. Pierce, *Supplication,* 1950. Oil, 18 x 24 inches.

John T. Riddle, Jr.

John Riddle's work is extremely strong yet sensitive and deals with black America. He recently lectured at the Los Angeles County Art Museum on the current phenomena in black art as related to great social protest artists of the past.

Of his "American Dream" series, two paintings of which are represented here, Riddle writes: "This attempts to depict the restless dream tormented sleep of the black bedroom. Discarded metal and other found objects along with inner-city scenes are used to create the images, sometimes hopeful, at other times nightmarish. The tired ghetto dweller wearily falls across his bed . . . to sleep, perhaps to dream."

Riddle, a native of California, was born in 1933, attended Los Angeles City College, and is a graduate of California State College, Los Angeles. He is currently teaching art at Los Angeles High School.

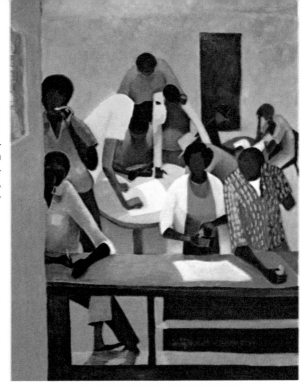

John T. Riddle, Jr.,
Saturday Morning,
1969. Oil on canvas,
48 x 36 inches. Col-
lection of the Golden
State Mutual Life In-
surance Company,
Los Angeles, Cali-
fornia.

John T. Riddle,
Jr., *Patriots Parade,*
1969. Oil on canvas,
31 x 24 inches.

Gregory D. Ridley, Jr.

Gregory D. Ridley, Jr. is a native of Smyrna, Tennessee. He holds a B.S. in art from Tennessee State University (1951) and an M.A. in art from the University of Louisville (1955). He has also done work in sculpture techniques. Ridley has been the recipient of many prizes and awards, a number of them from Atlanta University. He has also won the John Hope Landscape Award, the Gold Medal Award in Sculpture from the New York American Veterans Society Exhibition, and the second prize in sculpture — Emancipation Proclamation Award. Ridley's work has been exhibited throughout the United States. He is represented in Cedric Dover's *American Negro Art* (1961), *Famous Negroes Past and Present* (1967), and *Prize-Winning Art* (1965–68).

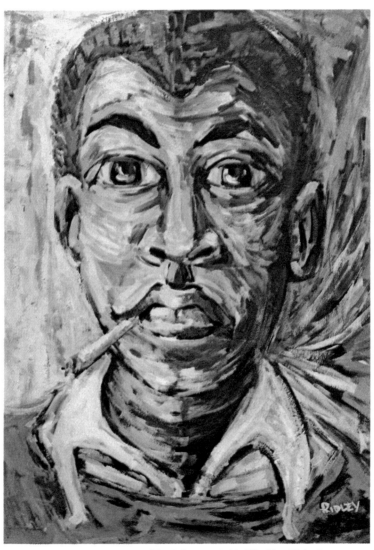

Gregory D. Ridley, Jr., *Black Power,* 1968. Oil, 22 x 30 inches.

Lucille Roberts

Lucille Roberts has had her work exhibited at Howard University (Washington, D.C.), the Society of Washington Artists, the Washington Gallery of Art, and the College Museum, Hampton (Virginia) Institute. Among her awards and honors are the Agnes Meyer Fellowship, and the First Prize Award of the Society of Washington Artists. A number of her paintings are on loan to the U.S. Department of State for their "Art in the Embassies" program.

She was born in Washington, D.C., and holds a B.A. from Howard University and an M.A. from the University of Michigan. She has done postgraduate work at Catholic University (Washington, D.C.), the Parson's School of Design (New York), and the Académie de la Grande Chaumière (Paris).

Lucille Roberts, *Black Heritage,* 1969. Acrylic painting, 42 x 48 inches.

Lucille Roberts, *Black Madonna,* 1969. Acrylic painting, 42 x 48 inches.

Arthur Rose

Arthur Rose is a native of Charleston, South Carolina. He received a B.A. degree in art from Claflin College (Orangeburg, South Carolina), and an M.A. degree from New York University (1952). He has done postgraduate work at New York University and at Indiana University.

His works have been exhibited at the Parthenon (Nashville, Tennessee), the Contemporary Art Gallery (Winston-Salem, North Carolina), Wesleyan University (Lincoln, Nebraska), and Atlanta University.

Mr. Rose's awards include an honorable mention from Kings Cotton Mills (Lancaster, South Carolina), J. O. Endris & Son Jewelers (New Albany, Indiana) Silver Trophy "Best in Show" award, the Orangeburg and New Town Player second-prize award.

He has had one-man shows at Lycoming College (Williamsport, Pennsylvania), Café La Tortilla (Bloomington, Indiana), Stillman College (Tuscaloosa, Alabama), North Carolina A.&T. State University (Greensboro), and the Columbia (South Carolina) Museum of Art First Invitational 1969. Rose's work is represented in the Indiana University collection.

He is presently chairman of the art department at Claflin College.

Arthur Rose, *The Family*, 1969. Oil, 24 x 36 inches.

Nancy Rowland

Nancy Rowland was born in 1945 in Los Angeles, studied at the Art Center College of Design in Los Angeles, and was graduated from San Jose State College. She is currently assistant art director at Botsford Ketchum, a Los Angeles advertising agency.

Nancy Rowland, *Sunset,* 1967. Oil on canvas, 48 x 48 inches. On loan from the artist.

Marion Sampler

A member of the Art Directors Club of Los Angeles, Marion Sampler has had his works exhibited in the Los Angeles County Art Museum, the Los Angeles Art Association, Long Beach State College, and the Rex Evans Gallery (Los Angeles).

He was born in Anniston, Alabama, in 1922 and has studied at the Art Academy of Cincinnati, the Jepson Art Institute (Los Angeles), and the University of Southern California (Los Angeles). He is currently head of the graphics department for Gruen Associates in Los Angeles.

Marion Sampler, *Untitled*,
1968. Oil, 48 x 48 inches.
On loan from the artist.

Marion Sampler, *Untitled*,
1965. Oil, 72 x 72 inches.
Collection of Radoslav L.
Sutnar, Los Angeles, California.

Raymond Saunders

Raymond Saunders was born in Pittsburgh in 1934; he has studied at the University of Pennsylvania, the Pennsylvania Academy of the Fine Arts (Philadelphia), the Barnes Foundation (Philadelphia), and the Carnegie Institute of Technology (Pittsburgh). He holds an M.F.A. from the California College of Arts and Crafts (Oakland).

His awards include a National Scholastic Scholarship, Pennsylvania Academy Scholarships, the Cresson European Traveling Scholarship, the National Institute of Arts and Letters Award, a Ford Foundation Purchase Award, the Schwabacker-Frey Award, (San Francisco, California), and the Prix de Rome.

He has exhibited at the Terry Dintenfass Gallery in New York (one-man shows), the San Francisco Museum of Art, the Pennsylvania Academy of the Fine Arts, the Philadelphia Art Museum, and has had several group exhibitions at the New School (New York).

Saunders' work appears in the collections of the Whitney Museum of American Art, the Pennsylvania Academy of the Fine Arts, the Allentown (Pennsylvania) Art Museum, Howard University (Washington, D.C.), California College of Arts and Crafts, the Addison Gallery of American Art (Andover, Massachusetts), and in many private collections throughout the United States, Mexico, and Europe.

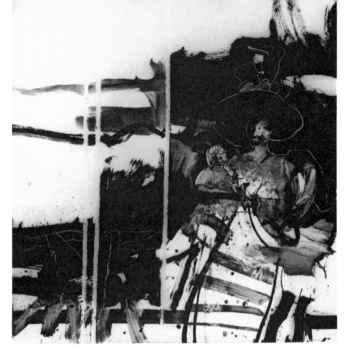

Raymond Saunders, *Three,* 1967. Oil, 75 x 79 inches. Reprinted courtesy of the Terry Dintenfass Gallery, New York.

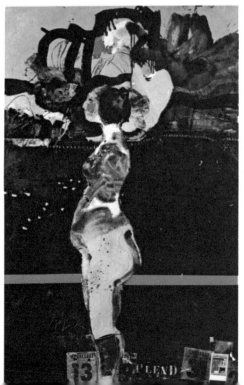

Raymond Saunders, *Plendalove,* 1967. Oil-collage, 82 x 52 inches. Collection of Rabbi and Mrs. Samuel Glaser. Reprinted courtesy of the Terry Dintenfass Gallery, New York.

Jewel Woodward Simon

Jewel Simon's interest in art began as a hobby which led to study with many independent artists and at Atlanta University. Additional study included a Certificate of Graduation from Art Instruction, Inc., and a bachelor of fine arts degree from the Atlanta School of Art.

Mrs. Simon is a native of Houston, Texas. She graduated from Atlanta University with honors, receiving her bachelor of arts degree.

She has exhibited extensively and has won many prizes in oil, watercolor, and sculpture, particularly at the Atlanta University Annual Art Exhibition. She has had her works exhibited in Texas, New York, California, Leipzig, Leningrad, and Moscow, as well as in many local showings. Many of Mrs. Simon's works are included in private collections throughout the United States and in Sierre Leone, Guyana, and New Zealand.

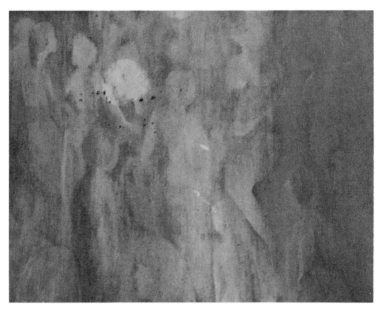

Jewel W. Simon, *Apparition,* 1969. 30 x 40 inches.

Vincent D. Smith

Leaving school at age sixteen, Vincent Smith traveled throughout the northeast while working for the Lackawanna Railroad. After serving in the Army, he turned to art and studied under Reginald Marsh at the Art Students League and with Joseph Kongal at the Brooklyn Museum Art School. In 1955 Smith was awarded a scholarship to the Skowhegan School in Maine, where he studied with Ben Shahn and Sidney Simon. He has had numerous one-man shows and has been awarded a John Hay Whitney Fellowship, and a grant-in-art by the National Institute of Arts and Letters.

Smith served as artist-in-residence at the Smithsonian Conference Center, Elkridge, Maryland, in 1967.

In 1969 he was represented in a one-man show at The Studio Museum in Harlem.

A native of Brooklyn, Smith was born there in 1929.

Vincent D. Smith, *Black Caucus,* 1969. Oil and sand on canvas, 30 x 30 inches. Reprinted courtesy of the Lacardia Gallery, New York.

Alma W. Thomas

Alma Thomas was born in Columbus, Georgia, and received a B.S. in fine arts from Howard University (Washington, D.C.) and an M.A. in art education from Columbia University.

Her work has appeared in over seventy group art shows and numerous one-woman shows. Miss Thomas has received many honors, among them an exhibition of her painting in both the Washington, D.C.'s mayor's office and the White House (1969). She is represented in *Who's Who in American Women, Who's Who in American Artists,* and Cedric Dover's *American Negro Art.* Her works are part of the Howard University collection, the George Washington University Art Gallery (Washington, D.C.), and many private collections.

Alma W. Thomas, *Spring Scene in Washington,* 1968. Acrylic, 40 x 40 inches.

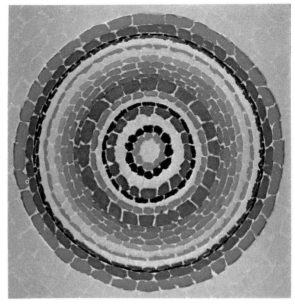

Alma W. Thomas, *An Impression of the Azaleas in the National Arboretum,* 1968. Acrylic, 60 x 50 inches.

Leo F. Twiggs

A native of St. Stephen, South Carolina, Leo Twiggs received his B.A. from Claflin College (Orangeburg, South Carolina), and an M.A. from New York University. He has studied at the Art Institute of Chicago and is currently a doctoral candidate in art education at the University of Georgia as well as an assistant professor of art at South Carolina State College.

His work has been exhibited at Atlanta University, Indiana University, the Mint Museum (Charlotte, North Carolina), the Old Slave Mart Museum (Charleston, South Carolina), the University of Georgia, Lincoln University (Jefferson City, Missouri), South Carolina State College, and the Columbia (South Carolina) Museum of Art.

His paintings appear in the collections of Atlanta University, South Carolina State College, the Charlotte Model Cities Program, the American Craftsman's Council (New York), and in many private collections.

In 1969 Twiggs was named an Outstanding Young Man of America for his accomplishments in teaching art to disadvantaged students.

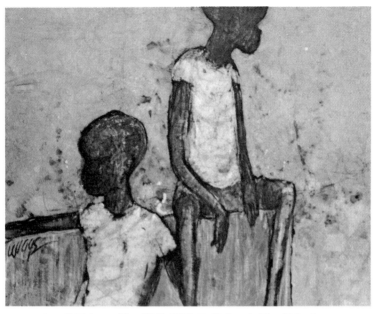

Leo F. Twiggs, *Blue Wall,* 1969. Batik (wax), 22 x 28 inches.

Royce H. Vaughn

Royce Vaughn is project director for Project ABLE (The Arts and Business Experiences). His work has been exhibited at San Francisco's Able I Art Gallery, Gilbert's Gallery, and the Blackman's Gallery. He has had shows at the Walnut Creek (California) Art Center, the Oakland Museum, San Francisco State College, and the Bank of America (San Francisco).

Vaughn is a frequent participant on panel shows and has produced two important documentary films: "The Street," about Fillmore Street in San Francisco, and "The Afro-American Thing," a film which has as its major goal the presentation and stimulation of the considerable tradition and resources of black artistic talent.

Vaughn was born in Cleveland, Ohio, in 1930. He attended Princeton University on a scholarship, holds a B.A. from San Francisco State College, and is currently working toward his master's degree.

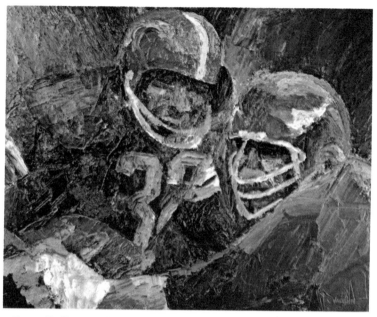

Royce H. Vaughn, *Autumn Muscle,* 1963. Oil on canvas, 38 x 50 inches.

James Watkins

James Watkins was born in Macon, Georgia, in 1925 and educated in Detroit. Since youth he has always been extremely sensitive to the plight of the black man in America, a sensitivity which is effectively portrayed in his work.

Watkins' paintings have appeared in six Annual Atlanta Exhibitions and each time have been honored with an award. He is represented in Cedric Dover's *American Negro Art.*

James Watkins, *Guitar Blues,* 1962. Oil, 27 x 37 inches.

Charles White

Charles White was born in Chicago in 1918. He studied at the Art Institute of Chicago, the Art Students League (New York), and at Taller de Grafica (Mexico City), and holds an honorary Ph.D. in arts from Columbia College, Chicago. He is on the executive board of the Black Academy of Arts and Letters. White has been the recipient of the Art Institute of Chicago Scholarship, two Julius Rosenwald Fellowships, a John Hay Whitney Fellowship, the Childe Hassam Award from the American Academy of Art, numerous Atlanta University Awards, Gold Medals from the International Show (Germany), a grant from the National Institute of Arts and Letters, and awards from the American Negro Exposition (Chicago), and the Metropolitan Museum of Art.

Among his almost countless exhibitions have been those at Howard University (Washington, D.C.), the Library of Congress, the University of Chicago, the Newark Museum, the Brooklyn Museum, the San Francisco Museum of Art, the Metropolitan Museum of Art, the Smithsonian Institute, the Oakland Art Museum, Karlovy Vary (Czechoslovakia), the Palace of Culture (Warsaw, Poland), the Pushkin Museum (Moscow), the Hermitage Museum (Leningrad), Ludwigshafen am Rhein (Germany), the University of Wisconsin, the National Center of Afro-American Artists, and the Forum Gallery, New York.

His work is in the collections of Atlanta University, Howard University, the Tuskegee Institute, the Deutsche Academie der Kunste (Berlin), the Dresden (Germany) Museum of Art, the Hirshhorn Collection (Washington, D.C.), the Government of Ghana, the Oakland Art Museum, and in the private collections of Mrs. Nat (King) Cole, the late Lorraine Hansberry, Sidney Poitier, Harry Belafonte, Gordon Parks, Bill Cosby, Jr., and *Ebony* magazine.

White's illustrations have appeared in many books, and his work has been the subject of at least a dozen publications.

Charles White, *Nat Turner, Yesterday, Today, & Tomorrow*, 1968. Ink, 51 x 78 inches. Collection of National Center of Afro-American Artists, Boston, Massachusetts. Reprinted courtesy of the Heritage Gallery, Los Angeles, California.

Charles White, *Two Alone*, 1946. Oil, 29 x 25 inches. Negro Collection, Atlanta University.

Garrett Whyte

Of his work Garrett Whyte writes:

> My art is based primarily on man, his environment
> and the physical, and spiritual relationship
> to the universal concept.
> The subject matter is predominantly Black.
> I began working with said forms in 1960 . . . for
> I believe the symbol of Black consciousness
> is "The Chosen" of this age.
> I also paint religious works, in terms of
> applicability of the *now* of our existence.

Whyte's paintings have been exhibited in one-man shows at South
Side Community Art Center and the First Federal Gallery (Chicago);
and in group shows at the International Gallery (Chicago) and the
Waller Gallery, Hyde Park (Chicago); the University of Southern
Illinois (Carbondale); the University of Chicago; and the University
of Illinois, Circle Campus (Chicago).

His works are also in the collections of the Illinois Bell Telephone
Company, and the Seeberg Corporation in Chicago.

A two-color spread of Garrett Whyte's paintings appeared in the
Chicago Sun-Times magazine, *Mid-West,* and a reproduction of a
work was published in *Art Gallery,* an international magazine.

Garrett Whyte, *They Went North,* 1966. Oil, 34 x 38 inches.

John Wilson

John Wilson was born in Boston in 1922. He holds a B.S. in education from Tufts University (Medford, Massachusetts), and has studied at Fernand Léger's School (Paris), the Institute Politecnico (Mexico City), and the Escuela de las Artes del Libro (Mexico City). He is currently an associate professor at Boston University.

Wilson's awards include Atlanta University's John Hope Award, the James William Paige Traveling Fellowship, the John Hay Whitney Fellowship, the Best Lithograph Award of the Silvermine Guild, and a Merit Citation from the Society of Illustrators' National Exhibit.

Wilson's work has been exhibited widely, and a number of his prints and paintings are owned by the Boston Public Library, the Museum of Modern Art, Atlanta University, the Carnegie Institute of Technology (Pittsburgh), the Bezalel Museum (Jerusalem), Howard University (Washington, D.C.), Tufts University, the Rose Museum of Brandeis University (Waltham, Massachusetts), as well as by many private collectors.

He has illustrated three books to date and is listed in *Who's Who in American Art.*

John Wilson, *Roxbury Rooftops,* 1954. Watercolor, 41 x 30 inches. Negro Collection, Atlanta University.

Charles A. Young

Charles A. (Chuck) Young was born in 1930 and educated in the public school system of New York City. He did his undergraduate work in art at Hampton (Virginia) Institute, where he received a B.S. degree in art education and social science. He had further training in art at New York University, where his painting was done under the tutelage of Hale Woodruff. Young received his master of arts degree at Catholic University (Washington, D.C.), where he studied painting and printmaking.

He is presently an associate professor of art at Federal City College, Washington, D.C.

He has had his work exhibited in the Richmond (Virginia) Museum of Art, the Honeycutt Art Exhibition (Fayetteville, North Carolina), and the Washington, D.C., Art Festival. In 1962 his work won first and second prizes in the Annual Art Exhibition in Fayetteville. Two of his paintings are presently traveling with the Fisk University collection.

Charles A. Young, *Ghetto Mother & Daughter,* 1968. Oil, 36 x 50 inches.

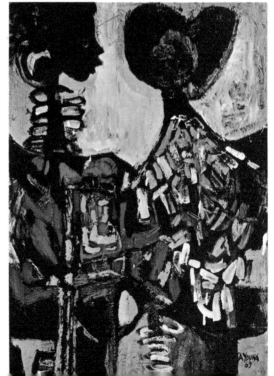

Charles A. Young, *Dansikis Madonnas,* 1969. Oil, 40 x 51 inches.